"May I Please Speak With My Father?"

A From My Heart to Yours Publication

"May I Please Speak With My Father?"

An Interactive Journal on Reconnecting with Our Heavenly Father

Editor: Jeannine Nyangira
Illustrator: James Steele

A From My Heart to Yours Publication

Be Magnified by Lynn Deshazo
©1992 Integrity's Hosanna! Music/ASCAP
c/o Integrity Media, Inc., 1000 Cody Road, Mobile, AL 36695

SAN 255-6774

ISBN 1-932721-99-1

Conversation is a Dialogue...

Why an interactive journal? Because the challenges, trials, and victories that we experience are not just about us. When we share our testimonies and the things on our hearts, we always minister to those around us. As others hear our testimonies, they will be freed and ready to share with someone else so that they, too, can be free to share with others.

Conversation is a dialogue, and this book acts like a dialogue on paper. When Jeannine, one of my friends and contributors to this book, gave me feedback on its first draft, she wrote:

I always kind of picture a bunch of women in a coffee shop just talking and meditating on this. In school, we talked about "discourse communities"— groups that exchange ideas. And that's what this text is—a discourse community—almost like a conversation taking place before your eyes. Sometimes I think we feel so alone in our situations, and that's a myth this text dispels big-time.

This book contains various journal entries, verses, letters, and thoughts. My prayer is that my thoughts — and the thoughts of others — would encourage you to pursue a deeper relationship with our Father. This will bring healing and deliverance, which will allow you to open your heart and share your own thoughts. Hopefully, it will stir up discussion with friends in a study group or, even better, open up a line of communication with you and your heavenly and earthly fathers. After all, our Father is the best conversationalist of them all.

This is from my heart to yours.

Dedication

When I needed encouragement: "You're doing a super job, lady!"

When I felt alone or that no one understood: "Baby, until someone has walked a mile in your shoes, they can't say anything to ya.'"

When I accomplished even the smallest task: "Yippee! You're a winner!"

For all of his love and encouragement, I am so thankful. How can I thank You, Lord, for placing me in my father-in-law's life for a season? I am forever grateful.

In memory of William "Papa Will" Davis

1922-2002

Acknowledgements

To my heavenly Father: Thank You for loving me. You have shown me mercy and grace time and time again. You are a loving, compassionate, and giving Daddy.

To my husband, Steve: Thank you for always encouraging me and pushing me beyond what I thought I could ever do! Thank you for being a visionary. God has used you to show me how to dream dreams and have visions. Every time I look at you, I thank God that you chose me to be your wife. Thank you for being the father of our seven wonderful children. I look forward to growing old with you!

To my children: Steve Jr., Jessica, Angel, Joshua, David, William, and Tabitha. I love you very much. God continues to use you to teach me some of life's greatest lessons.

To my mommy: I love you, Mommy! Thank you for still treating me like I'm your baby. I need you, and I have risen up to bless you!

To my pastor, Thelma Leftwich, a woman after God's own heart: God has used you to stretch me in ways I didn't know I could be stretched. The things God has told you to speak into my spirit have literally saved my life.

To the praying women of Vessels of His Love Church: my dream has become a reality because of your prayers!

To Jeannine Nyangira: Thank you for being my daughter, sister, friend, and editor. Thank you for always holding my arms up and telling me I could do anything! What a blessing that we flow together!

Contents

Part One — Our Earthly Fathers

My Thoughts: "May I Please Speak With my Father?" ....Preface

Others' Thoughts: Intro (By Pastor Thelma Leftwich) 3

My Thoughts: "Hi Beautiful!" 4

Others' Thoughts: Just to Be In His Presence
(By Pastor Thelma Leftwich)................................5

My Thoughts: Letter to an Earthy Father 6

God's Thoughts: I Kings 19:11-12 7

Others' Thoughts: My Father's Voice is the Voice of God's
(By Gail Krahenbuhl)...8

Your Thoughts: Journaling Moment...10

God's Thoughts: Psalm 27:10 11

Others' Thoughts: Nick (By Jeannine Nyangira) 12

God's Thoughts: Joel 2:25 14

Others' Thoughts: God Can Truly Restore the Years the
Cankerworm Has Stolen (By Janice Johnson) 15

Your Thoughts: Journaling Moment 17-18

Part Two — Our Heavenly Father

God's Thoughts: Romans 8:15 21

My Thoughts: Choosing Not to Walk in Fear 22

God's Thoughts: Proverbs 3:12 23

My Thoughts: Perception and No Connection 24

God's Thoughts: Psalm 34:5 26

My Thoughts: Love Covers a Multitude of Faults........................27

Your Thoughts: Journaling Moment 28

My Thoughts: My Daddy Owns Everything 29

Others' Thoughts: "Be Magnified" (By Lynn DeShazo) 30

My Thoughts: Apart From Him I Can Do Nothing 31

God's Thoughts: II Kings 3:7-9...32

My Thoughts: I Aim to Please Only Him 33

My Thoughts: My Daddy Is Big, Strong, And Mighty! 34

My Thoughts: My Father Is a Buffer 36

My Thoughts: Perfection...37

Your Thoughts: Journaling Moment 38

My Thoughts: Letter to a Heavenly Father 39

God's Thoughts: John 20:17 40

My Thoughts: He Is Not a Man 41

My Thoughts: Image Bearer 42

Your Thoughts: Journaling Moment 43

Part Three—Extended Journal Section

Preface

"May I Please Speak With My Father?"

I will never forget hearing my son David speak those words to his father's secretary, words that triggered something deep within my spirit:

"Hello. May I please speak with Steve Davis?"

"Steve is busy at the moment. May I please take a message?"

"Tell him it is his son, David. *Let me speak with my father!*"

Such authority. Without a doubt, he knew he had access that few had. All because he was in the bloodline, he had the access. As I listened, the old pain and insecurity once again returned — that feeling of being separated and disconnected from my heavenly Father. Although I had grasped the fact that He had sent Jesus, His only son, to die for me, this father-daughter relationship wasn't something that could be understood. Something was missing from my life. The idea that I could ask for my father with that boldness only brought fear to my spirit. How could I heal that area in my life? Was I the only one out there who needed understanding of who Father God was? Did anyone else need to understand that connection? Where could I start?

This book was written to explore these questions together. To some, it will be a devotional. To others, it will give understanding. To still others, it will be a source of healing and strength. Most of all, it will help you understand that your Father loves you very much and desires to have a personal relationship with you, made possible through the shed blood of our Lord and Savior, Jesus Christ. It will give you the opportunity to share your heart about your earthly and heavenly fathers, and other women will share about their relationships, too. As you communicate with God and the others in this book, you will realize that you do have access to your heavenly Father.

Part One

Our Earthly Fathers

Others' Thoughts

"In pastoral counseling, we were trained to ask our clients,
'What kind of relationship do you have with your father?' It was the
key to knowing how to handle the root of some of their problems."

Pastor Thelma Leftwich

My Thoughts

"Hi, Beautiful!"

These are words often heard in this home, words that the girls always hear from their father. They don't understand the words now, but they will never question what their father thinks of them. They will know that they are created in the image and likeness of God, and for that reason, they lack nothing. They will not look for anyone else to fill that void in their life.

I always imagine someone trying to someday court my daughters. Mere flowers or words of praise will never do, because they already get those from their father. While these things are nice to receive, they can become a snare when you've never received them and are looking for something to fill a hole in your life. However, when words are used in proper context, they can be life and healing. My daughters are full to overflowing with love and those two little words: "Hi, Beautiful!"

Others' Thoughts

Just to Be in His Presence

Pastor Thelma Leftwich

I was close to my earthly father. I loved him very much, and the memories that I have of him did draw me closer to my heavenly Father. My father worked for the railroad, and I could not wait until he would get home. I would run to meet him and would be greeted with so much love and plenty of hugs. I remember sitting on our porch swing with him and being so happy. I marveled at his words of wisdom, words that still influence my life today. Anytime I could be with him, I was happy. I loved to sit in his presence. He didn't have to say a word; just being in his presence was enough.

My Thoughts

Dear Dad,

It's with great joy that I write this letter. I hope that as you read this book, it will not make you sad. I want to tell you that I love you. It's not the type of love that came from being "daddy's little girl." It's the kind of love that comes from our Lord. I'm happy to say that we both serve that same Lord, so you understand whom I am referring to.

For so long when I watched Steve minister to the girls, I felt anger. He always knows what to say to them, but I believed it was a little extreme because I didn't understand. I would try every way to hinder him from loving the girls freely. Then the Holy Spirit began to show me that I was jealous of my own daughters. How ugly is that? That's when the eyes of my understanding were opened, and I began to consider a father's role.

As you have gotten older, your heart has become so tender, and you've tried to reach out to me. But because I was angry, I decided I'd withhold my love from you. The very thing I had prayed for was happening: that God would change your heart and that He'd also put you in a church where you'd be taught the Word of God. He did that, and then I couldn't receive it. But God has changed my heart, Dad. I now realize that you did the best you could do. God has ministered to me by showering me with His love. Scripture says, "He who is forgiven much, loves much." I love you, Dad.

I have to share my favorite memory of you. When we went to church together not that long ago, I remember closing my eyes and raising my hands in surrender to God during praise and worship. Then I looked up and saw your hands raised, too. I thought that could never happen. But I underestimated the power of God. We worshiped our Lord together! I will never forget that, and I know it will be the first of many times.

I love you Dad, and I thank God that my kids have a grandfather like you.

Your daughter,

Tanya Davis (forever your T.J.)

God's Thoughts

The Lord said,
"Go out and stand on the mountain in the presence of the Lord,
for the Lord is about to pass by."
Then a great and powerful wind tore the mountains apart
and shattered the rocks before the Lord,
but the Lord was not in the wind.
After the wind there was an earthquake,
but the Lord was not in the earthquake.
After the earthquake came a fire,
but the Lord was not in the fire.
And after the fire came a gentle whisper.

I Kings 19:11-12

My Father's Voice is the Voice of God's
Gail Krahenbuhl

When I was a little girl, my dad left the country for about a month to minister the Gospel. Although I'd been active before, I wouldn't eat, became listless, and had no interest in life. When my mom took me to the doctor, he concluded that I was suffering from a broken heart, because my daddy was gone. That pain had physically manifested itself in my body. When my dad returned, I clung to him. I was okay, because I wanted him with me. I wanted him to be close by.

Although I'm now a married woman with children, when it comes to my father, I still feel like a little girl when I'm around him. This especially happens when we don't agree. As an adult, I have opinions about some things, and my dad, who's a pastor, has his own opinions. Sometimes the way he interprets the Scriptures may not be the way I see it. Where I may see shades of gray in a situation, with him it's black or white. It's during these times when I realize how badly I want him to validate me. I hate to disappoint him; I want his approval.

As I grew up, I knew that if my dad disapproved of someone I wanted to marry, I wouldn't marry that person. I wouldn't want to disappoint my dad. But I also believe that if I had gone ahead and disobeyed him, I would've been setting up my life for failure. In dating situations, my emotions were so heavily involved; I didn't trust myself to totally hear from God clearly, and I believe that my dad did. I knew he heard the voice of God.

However, now that I've grown, I sometimes struggle with knowing when my father's voice is the voice of God's. My father's voice is loving yet also forceful and strong. And I think my siblings also share this conflict with me, so we can ask each other, "What's going on here? Who is who?" And we siblings also have our spouses, who kind of fall into this struggle, too. They're conflicted as well, because all of my in-laws have also made my father their spiritual father. Still, our spouses have some emotional distance on this, since he's not their literal dad. They don't have all the stuff from childhood, all that history. They're just close enough to each of us to help us analyze it. All four of us have needed our spouses who deeply honor our dad, but who can also be objective. But I'm not comfortable doing that with anyone outside of the family. Since I'm fiercely loyal to my dad, I wouldn't just call up one of my girlfriends to talk about him.

Scripturally, I know I have the right to leave my father and cleave to my husband. And my father tries to honor that. When we got married, he was the first one to tell our spouses, "I'm no longer the first man in their lives; you are." He may even be relieved that he doesn't have the full brunt of being the priest in the home anymore, because he takes that seriously. And without discussing this with him, I think it could be somewhat of a burden. I know that now as a parent. But he's still very much there to give his opinions when he feels they're warranted. And so we have to sift through that.

Finally, it helps that I look at my father differently when he's speaking in the office of the pastorate. Then it's easier to separate who is speaking: father or pastor. When he's giving me direction or guidance, it can be tough. I ask myself, "Is that my heavenly Father speaking, or my earthly father?" But when my dad says, "The Lord is telling me this," I know that the Lord is speaking through him. He's not only my father but also my pastor. This makes him my spiritual leader.

True, it's been a struggle. Two important voices that are sometimes hard to tell apart. But I don't think I'd struggle so much with this if I didn't love him so dearly.

Your Thoughts

As a child, did you receive an abundance of love from your dad?

_____

_____

_____

Talk about how your dad encouraged you as a child. How have those words benefited you as an adult?

_____

_____

_____

Share a special father-daughter moment. If there were not any special moments, talk about how you feel about that.

_____

_____

_____

_____

_____

God's Thoughts

Even when my mother and father forsake me, the Lord will receive me.

Psalm 27:10

Others' Thoughts

Nick

Jeannine Nyangira

Sometimes what you have to forgive is an absence, not a presence. I never knew my father — or Nick, as I call him — but I knew what he had done to our family. During my childhood nights, I'd lie in Mama's bed on the other side of the world from where she'd birthed me, and I'd listen to stories of Why It Didn't Work Out. In my little afro-topped head, I kept a list of questions for Nick. They went like this:

1. Why did you drink so much?
2. Where did you really go at night?
3. Why did you push us so much that we finally had to leave?
4. (Return to #1 and repeat questions for the next 20 years.)

Out of concern for my safety, we never told Nick exactly where we lived. When we fled Kenya for Mama's home state of Nebraska in 1974, we slipped under the radar and never saw Nick again. Ah, but I did see him — in the mirror, in my naptime dreams, in the way I *hated* Father's Day, and in the way Mama's face would strain as she balanced her checkbook. As I grew, Nick appeared in how my body tensed up if I came within a foot and a half from males. I didn't know what to do with them. I didn't know what to do with him. But I had an example to follow, an ironic mentor: Mama. Never in all her painful stories had she displayed bitterness, and she was the one who'd actually lived through it all. Observing her forgiveness in action, I thought she had to be either very naïve or extremely wise. Eventually, I realized she was free.

Could I do this? Could I hold my abandonment in both hands — not denying its pain — and yet with those same hands reach out to my father, lay hands on his memory, and bless him? Eventually I realized I had to. For him, for me, for the Author of forgiveness Himself.

During my senior year in college, I learned that Nick had died. I don't know if he did so with my name on his lips or if I had long since faded from his conscience. But I do pray that somehow he knew that his daughter would eventually say, "All right. Be at peace, Nick. Be at peace."

God's Thoughts

And I will restore to you the years that the locust hath eaten, the cankerworm, and the caterpillar, and the palmerworm...

Joel 2:25

God Can Truly Restore the Years the Cankerworm Has Stolen

Janice Johnson

The seventh of eleven children, I come from a very close family that shared a three-room house and a large yard for playing. Having so many siblings who fought for our parents' attention was pretty tough. I always felt that my younger brothers and sisters were more important than me and deserved our parents' attention. I don't know why, but I still do that today.

Our mom was always at home caring for us, but our dad was hardly ever at home. He worked two jobs and frequented bars and clubs on the weekends. As a child, I spent time with my dad on Sundays, sitting at his feet and watching sports on TV. I developed an interest in football, because it allowed me time with my dad. Even though he didn't really show much interest in me, just being around him made me happy. I wanted to be around him for the time when he did recognize me. Looking back, I bet the seed of rejection was being planted.

Most of the memories of my childhood with my dad aren't pleasant. Although I wanted to be near him when he was at home, he usually ignored us. I now realize that I was looking for him to fill a void that only my heavenly Father could fill. I needed someone to point me to my heavenly Father; although my dad was the closest male adult around at that time, he was not capable of doing that.

One day, while watching my mother serve my dad like a slave, I said, "When I grow up, I will take care of my dad." At the time, I looked at my mother's position as a position of honor, because of the way I felt toward my dad.

When I was in middle school, my mother put my dad out of the house because of his abusive behavior towards her and my siblings. He found a place to live close to our house, and every day after school, my siblings and I would visit him. He would give us a lot of attention. He didn't have a choice, because no one else wanted to be around him because of his past behavior. He needed us; he was extremely lonely. Sometimes he would be mean to us, but I didn't care, because I was spending time with my dad.

While I was in high school, my dad was diagnosed with diabetes. This required him to have surgery a few times, including the amputation of his leg. After graduating from college, I came home to take care of my dad, and for the next fifteen years, became his caregiver. I devoted my life to caring for him. While doing so, I realized that I forgave him for all the past hurt and disappointment and began to truly love and respect him as my earthly father. This occurred as I became closer to my heavenly Father. All the hurts and old feelings disappeared. It was as if I lost my memory. It was a new beginning: God restored our relationship. No one could tell me anything bad about my dad that could pull up old wounds, because they were healed, and negative words could not change the love I felt for him.

During those years, my dad gave his life to Christ, and so did I. We now shared a heavenly Father and had lots to talk about. Loving my dad showed me how to love my heavenly Father, and in a way, my dad led the way for me to the Father. He did this by exemplifying Christ-like behavior. I had the pleasure of spending good quality time with my dad, and during the last few years of his life was able to get from him all that I didn't receive from him while I grew up. All the years the cankerworm had stolen, my Father God restored.

Your Thoughts

Was your father around when you were a child?

_____

_____

_____

Was/is your dad a believer in the Lord Jesus Christ?

_____

_____

_____

Did you have a painful relationship with your earthly father? If so, how have you dealt with the pain? How has your heavenly Father ministered to you?

_____

_____

_____

_____

_____

_____

Your Thoughts

Write a letter to your earthly father, whether he is alive or not. You don't have to share it with him if he is alive; this just gives you an opportunity to share your feelings.

_____

_____

_____

_____

_____

_____

_____

_____

_____

_____

_____

_____

_____

_____

_____

_____

_____

_____

_____

Part Two

Our Heavenly Father

God's Thoughts

For we have not received a spirit of bondage to fear,
but we have received a spirit of adoption,
whereby we cry, "Abba, Father!"

Romans 8:15

My Thoughts

Choosing Not To Walk In Fear

For a long time, I associated God with fear. Fear involves punishment, and I always expected that I would be punished. But my Father's love is perfect. Scripture says, "Perfect love drives out all fear" (I John 4:18).

I remember being pregnant with my son Joshua, scared that God would punish me for past sexual sins. I thought something would be wrong with my son; surely this would be God's way of punishing me. But my Father, out of his mercy, brought forth a healthy baby boy.

Is my Father the judge of the universe? Yes, He is the judge of the universe. Do we reap what we sow? Yes, we reap what we sow. But does He desire to punish us? No, He doesn't. He honors our broken and repentant hearts. He sees them, and with compassion and love, looks at us through the blood of *His* son, Jesus Christ.

Just as an earthly parent, God has no desire to punish His children. We know when our children are truly repentant and when they're not. We also know what it will take to help them understand their errors, and our hearts are full of compassion when they do understand those errors. That's our Father! He sees our hearts and is moved with compassion when we are broken before him. Even though we understand He is a God of grace and compassion, we don't take advantage of Him. We respect His position and rest in His love.

God's Thoughts

For the Lord corrects those He loves,
just as a father corrects a child in whom He delights.

Proverbs 3:12

My Thoughts

Perception and No Connection

Father, it's amazing how our perception of You can become distorted. I repent, because I've placed You on the level with man. I've always been afraid of You, but I didn't fear You. I was like the children of Israel: when they heard Your voice from the mountain, they drew back, since they were afraid. It wasn't a fear from respect or awe; that kind of fear would have led them to be obedient. They were just scared and therefore drew back. But Moses drew nearer to You out of reverence. He respected You, and so He obeyed You. And You called Him "friend."

Lord Jesus, I've known that You came to this earth as a man and that our Father sent You to die for us because He loved us. That concept wasn't hard for me to grasp. You always pointed to our Father and always made sure everyone knew He was the reason You were being obedient. You became the mediator between God and man. But my fleshly fear kept me from understanding that this Father can be approached — that I can talk to Him, fellowship with Him, and love Him, and He will do the same with me. Because of His love, I can respect Him and please Him through obedience. Still, for so long, I had a perception of His love without its connection in my spirit.

My husband Steve is 6'2" and weighs 250 pounds. When he speaks, his voice thunders. And when he calls us by name, his voice carries no whimpering or timidity. Those who don't know him misunderstand his loud voice. If one of my friends were around when Steve came home, she'd get up and leave. (As a matter of fact, she wouldn't even come over if she knew Steve was home.) I never understood her fear of him, because I knew Steve's heart. Those of us who truly know him hold a different perception. When Steve loudly calls the kids by name, they unflinchingly reply, "Yes, Dad?" They understand that when called, they should immediately respond — not out of fear, but out of respect and love. One day, Steve had to correct our daughter at a game. Of course, she was angry and embarrassed. But when her friends said, "I'm scared of your dad!" she laughed and said, "That's funny. My dad is nothing but a pussycat!" How awesome this is — to understand the difference between fear and respect. It's awesome to be disciplined by your heavenly Father, yet to still know He is full of love. That's a connection that will give us more understanding of the Father's love.

God's Thoughts

Those who seek the Lord are radiant.
Their faces are never covered in shame.

Psalm 34:5

My Thoughts

Love Covers a Multitude of Faults

I tried pleasing my Father with works. Never worked! When I'd fall short, I knew He'd be disappointed in me. Instead of running into my Father's arms, I'd run away. I'd cut off our communication by not spending time with Him. After all, I'd made a mistake. He didn't want me around, anyway. His acceptance of me was something I couldn't deal with, because I never realized that someone could love me that much. I expected punishment but instead received chastisement with love. I received mercy. A new day every day. A new chance to start over.

Your Thoughts

When you relate to your heavenly Father, do you feel close and comfortable, or far away and fearful?

_____

_____

_____

_____

_____

_____

_____

Do you see your heavenly Father as punishing or merciful?

_____

_____

_____

_____

_____

_____

_____

My Thoughts

My Daddy Owns Everything

Can you imagine? The God of the universe is my daddy! He rules over everything. The heavens belong to Him, and the earth is His footstool. It's important to get down into my spirit how big He is, to take possession of the fact that He is my Father, to get Him off the earthly realm I have Him in. It's important that with my redirected fear I respect Him more than I did with my perverted fear. Lack of understanding. Unfocused mind. Giving the devil undeserved respect. Forgetting how big my Father truly is. Making Him small.

Be magnified, O Lord.

Others' Thoughts

By Lynn DeShazo

I have made You too small in my eyes
O Lord, forgive me
And I have believed in a lie
That You were unable to help me

But now, O Lord, I see my wrong
Heal my heart and show Yourself strong
And in my eyes and with my song
O Lord, be magnified
O Lord, be magnified

Be magnified, O Lord
You are highly exalted
And there is nothing You can't do
O Lord, my eyes are on you
Be magnified
O Lord, be magnified

My Thoughts

Apart From Him I Can Do Nothing

As the years go by, I've often thought, "I don't need a dad. I'm older now and can handle things." Then I feel overwhelmed and need to run into the arms of my Father. I need to cry, talk to Him, and receive His comfort.

God's Thoughts

…But I am like a child
who doesn't know his way around.
And here I am among Your own chosen people.
A nation so great they are too numerous to count!
Give me an understanding mind
so that I can govern Your people well
and know the difference
between right and wrong.

II Kings 3:7-9

(King's Solomon's prayer for wisdom.
In spite of his high position, he acknowledges that he needs the Father.)

My Thoughts

I Aim To Please Only Him

My father-in-law, Papa Will, was one of the most encouraging fathers I've known. Even if you couldn't tie your shoe correctly, as long as you tried, you'd hear him say, "Good job! You did your best." In fact, I found myself doing things just so he would notice. I felt like I needed his affirmation and felt empty when I didn't get his attention.

Man can't fill an area that only my Father can fill. If God doesn't fill it, it's a lonely spot that always has to be full of something. Positive as they were, Papa Will's affirmations were never enough; I always needed more. My heavenly Father would say to me, "That spot in your spirit that you keep trying to fill up with men's words belongs to Me. Let Me fill it up for you. You go here and there looking for the accolades of men, when all that is required of you is to be obedient to what I have called you to. Obedience will break the restlessness and will keep you from searching for men's praise. Obedience will release My glory. You will begin to look like Me and will begin to hear My voice when I am speaking."

When Jesus went to be baptized, the Father said, "This is My beloved Son, in Whom I am well pleased." What awesome words. To rest at the end of the day and hear my Father say, "I am pleased with you today." To know that when I miss it, I can still rest, because my Father gives me another chance. He loves me and will never leave me nor forsake me.

Father, may I have wisdom and understanding in my decision-making. May I make decisions based on the instructions I receive from You. Only Your voice, Father. Only Your instructions.

My Thoughts

My Daddy Is Big, Strong, And Mighty!

"My father is strong; he has lots of muscles!"

"Well, my dad is so big, he played pro football!"

"My dad picked me up with one hand when I fell down!"

Children see their dad as a giant. To them, Dad is big and strong. A child feels in awe in his presence. Boasting can lead to exaggerating; Dad always comes out as the conquering champion.

How do I place my heavenly Father above the image of man? How do I erase my fear that He'll disappoint me and let me down? I want Him to be big in my mind. I want Him to be my hero. I want Him to be the one to come and rescue me.

At age four, our son David was riding his bike in a neighborhood yard when he fell off, his foot stuck in the wheel. One of the neighborhood children ran over and cried, "Mr. and Mrs. Davis, David is hurt!" Before the words were even out of the child's mouth, my husband Steve jumped up, took off running, ran *through* the fence, and was at David's side. David is older now, but he still remembers how his father came to his rescue.

So many times Father God has come to my rescue, and my flippant attitude was, "He *should* come to my rescue. He *is* God." I never took it personally. I never appreciated that my Father, the God of the universe, comes to my rescue. He loves me just that much.

My Father is so strong; He opens up one hand and satisfies the desires of every living thing.

My Father is so strong; He establishes the boundaries in the ocean.

My Father is so powerful; He spoke the world into existence.

My Father is so powerful; He destroyed the world with floodwaters and started over again.

My Father is so holy that sin cannot stand in His presence.

My Father would do anything for me.

My Father has rescued me so many times that I've lost count.

My Father loves me so much that all I want to do is obey Him.

My Father has redeemed me…

My Thoughts

My Father Is a Buffer

He offers protection from the elements of this world. There are many things to be exposed to in this world, things meant to destroy us physically, mentally, emotionally, and spiritually. God's direction and wisdom serve as our protection. I think about times in my life when I believed that no one was there — things I would get myself into and things I easily could have gotten into.

Our girls often feel that their earthly father is hard on them. Right now in their young lives, they don't see the pain that they're being spared. They don't see that their father is a buffer but think he's a ruler, an authoritative figure who spoils the fun.

Our Father gives us free will. He won't force us to do anything we don't want to do. His principles are laid out to prevent pain, heartache, and scars. He sees the whole picture and knows where each road will take us. One day, my husband will have to let go and let our girls make their own choices. They will have to see that there is an even mightier voice than their father's that must be obeyed. They can choose to stay under the protection of their heavenly Father and keep on the narrow road of His precepts and principles, or they may attempt their own way — a wide, hard path with broken hearts and many, many scars.

My Thoughts

Perfection

It concerned me when the kids realized that their dad wasn't perfect, because I wanted them to believe that he'd never sinned. I've never wanted them to lose respect for their dad but to always honor him. However, I came to realize that they could end up making him a god and not realize how he's responsible to model Christ-like behavior and point them to God. At that moment when they realized he wasn't perfect, a temporary disconnect took place, but it was a necessary disconnect, because then they could connect with their heavenly Father. He can pour His love into their hearts, and as He does, they are able to love their earthly father even more. A healthier, stronger connection takes place. As He pours in, they receive and fall in love with their heavenly Father.

I remember once thinking, "But who do I receive from? How can I show my dad respect? It always seems, Lord, like a role reversal—that I am in the parental role. How do I honor my father as Your Word says to, because I believe that even as an adult child, I should honor my mother and father?" He said, "Let me pour My love into you, and as I do, you will be able to love your father. Why? Because then your focus will be directed from what your *father didn't* do to what *I did* for you."

I now have a reconnection with my earthly father and am able to love him freely. At times I've been angry because he can't give me what I think I need. But I have to remind myself how blessed I am to have love from my Father... the God of the universe.

Your Thoughts

Who are you to your heavenly Father?

_____

_____

_____

_____

_____

_____

_____

Do you believe that your relationship with your earthly father had any effect on how you respond to your heavenly Father?

_____

_____

_____

_____

_____

_____

_____

My Thoughts

Dear Dad,

I want to tell You that I love You. I thank You for taking care of me. For being patient with me. For molding me into a vessel fit for Your use. Thank You for protecting me, even when I was disobedient. You looked past all the sin and filth and saw that I just needed to be loved. You saw I was searching for You. You waited… I can hear You telling the devil, "Hands off! She belongs to Me. She's waddling right now, but she's Mine. I have a plan for her." You waited…

You didn't leave me in my polluted blood. When You saw me, You said, "Live, Tanya." You said, "I want you to have life. I want you to thrive like a plant in the field." Because of You, I've grown up into a beautiful jewel. You bathed me and washed me with Your blood and rubbed oil into my skin. You gave me expensive clothing of linen and silk, beautifully embroidered, and sandals made of fine leather. You gave me lovely jewelry: bracelets, necklaces, earrings, and a lovely crown for my head.

You've made me into a queen. I don't understand it, Lord. How can You love me so much? When it seemed that I didn't have a prayer, You called me "daughter." You called me unto Yourself. There is nothing to say but, "Thank You." Thank You for loving me with an everlasting love. I am forever grateful.

Your daughter,

Tanya Davis

God's Thoughts

I go home to be with your God and My God,
your Father and My Father.

John 20:17

(Jesus' words spoken before His ascension, showing us that we now share the same Father. Once we were disconnected from God, but Jesus wanted us to understand that we have been reconnected with our heavenly Father. Because of his death and resurrection, we now share the same Daddy!)

My Thoughts

He Is Not a Man

He loves you. His love is so great that He gave His only Son for you, since He hated being disconnected from you. Sometimes when a human disappoints us, we get a distorted view of our heavenly Father. We can't relate to Him; we shrink Him down to the standards of a man and forget how much He loves us. He is not flesh and blood. Our Father is the Lord God Almighty. The Lord God Almighty is your Daddy.

God's Thoughts

Image Bearer

Watermark:

A mark on paper that can be seen only when held up to the light.

Daughter,

I have loved thee with an everlasting love, and with compassion have I drawn thee unto Myself. When you fall, I am there to help you up. When you succeed, I am there to cheer you on. Nothing can separate you from My love. You are the apple of My eye. I designed and created you for a purpose. I have a plan. You are not a mistake. Before the foundation of the world, I saw you. I formed you and said, "It is good." I molded you and breathed My life into you.

So what do I need from you? Obedience. Obedience will release My glory. If you say that you love Me, you ought also to walk even as I walked. Diligently obey the Lord your God. You require it from your earthly children; I require it, also. You do have a choice, but remember that with obedience come blessings. It is my desire, daughter, to bless you with all that I have for you.

Will you choose the way I have for you, or will you choose your own way?

Your Thoughts

Write another letter to your earthly father. Based on anything your heavenly Father is showing you, is there anything else that you'd like to share with your earthly father?

_____

_____

_____

_____

_____

_____

_____

_____

_____

_____

_____

_____

_____

_____

_____

_____

_____

_____

Part Three

Extended Journal Section

Your Thoughts

Your Thoughts

Your Thoughts

Your Thoughts

Your Thoughts

Your Thoughts

Your Thoughts

Your Thoughts

_____

_____

_____

_____

_____

_____

_____

_____

_____

_____

_____

_____

_____

_____

_____

_____

_____

_____

Your Thoughts

Your Thoughts

Your Thoughts

Your Thoughts

Your Thoughts

Your Thoughts

Your Thoughts

Your Thoughts

Your Thoughts

Your Thoughts

Your Thoughts

Your Thoughts

Your Thoughts

Your Thoughts

Your Thoughts

Your Thoughts

Your Thoughts

Your Thoughts

Your Thoughts

Your Thoughts

Your Thoughts

Your Thoughts

Your Thoughts

Your Thoughts

Your Thoughts

Your Thoughts

Your Thoughts

Your Thoughts

Your Thoughts

Order Form

Email Orders: tanya@frommyheart.com

Phone orders: 630.452.2809

Postal orders: From My Heart to Yours Publishing
ATTN: Orders
2S685 Summerfield Ct.
Wheaton, IL 60187

Please send me _____ copies at $9.95 each to the following address:

Name: _____

Address:_____

City: _____ State: _____ Zip: _____

Email Address: _____

Postage & Handling: $3.00

Payment: ☐ Cash   ☐ Check

Thanks for your order!